D1441980

Explore Space!

Space Stations

by Gregory L. Vogt

Consultant:
James Gerard
Aerospace Education Specialist
NASA Aerospace Education Services Program

Bridgestone Books are published by Capstone Press
151 Good Counsel Drive, P.O. Box 669, Mankato, Minnesota 56002
http://www.capstone-press.com

Library of Congress Cataloging-in-Publication Data
Vogt, Gregory.
    Space stations/by Gregory L. Vogt.
    p. cm.—(Explore space!)
    Includes bibliographical references and index.
    Summary: Presents examples of space stations and explains how astronauts live
and work in them.
    ISBN 0-7368-0201-0
    1. Space stations—Juvenile literature. [1. Space stations. 2. Astronautics.] I. Title.
II. Series: Vogt, Gregory. Explore space!
TL797.15.V64 1999
629.44'2—DC21   98-45662
                                                                      CIP
                                                                      AC

Editorial Credits
Rebecca Glaser, editor; Steve Christensen, cover designer and illustrator; Kimberly
  Danger, photo researcher

Photo Credits
NASA, cover, 4, 6, 8, 10, 12, 14, 16, 18, 20

2 3 4 5 6 06 05 04 03 02 01

Table of Contents

Space Stations

Space stations are large spacecraft where astronauts live and work. Space stations orbit Earth. Astronauts can live in space stations for weeks or months at a time.

orbit
to travel around a planet

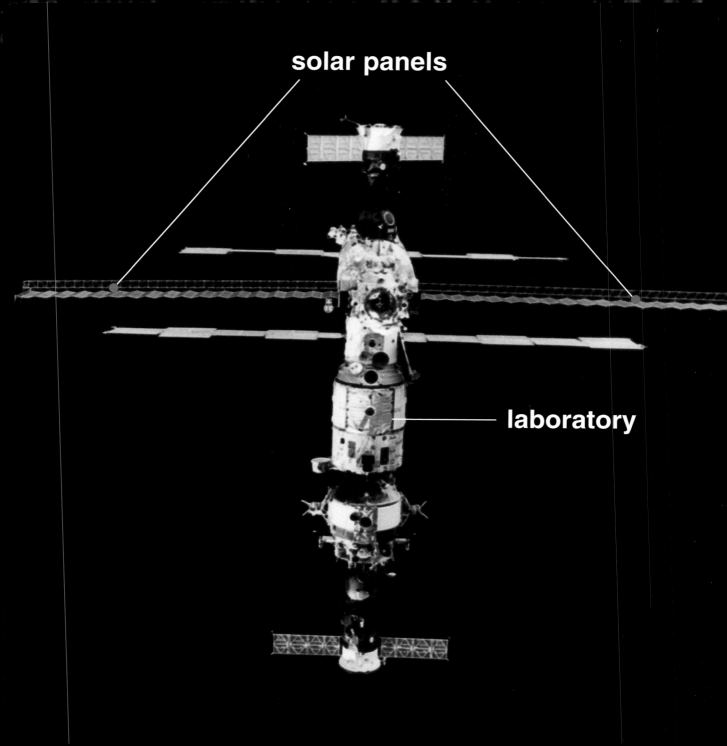

solar panels

solar panels

laboratory

Parts of Space Stations

Tunnels connect the sections of
space stations. Space stations have
laboratories where astronauts work.
Kitchens, bathrooms, and sleeping
rooms also are inside space stations.
Solar panels help power space stations.

solar panel
a flat surface that collects
sunlight and turns it into power

Working in Space

Astronauts do experiments to learn about space and Earth. Equipment covers the walls, floor, and ceiling of each laboratory. Astronauts use this equipment to learn how plants and animals grow in space.

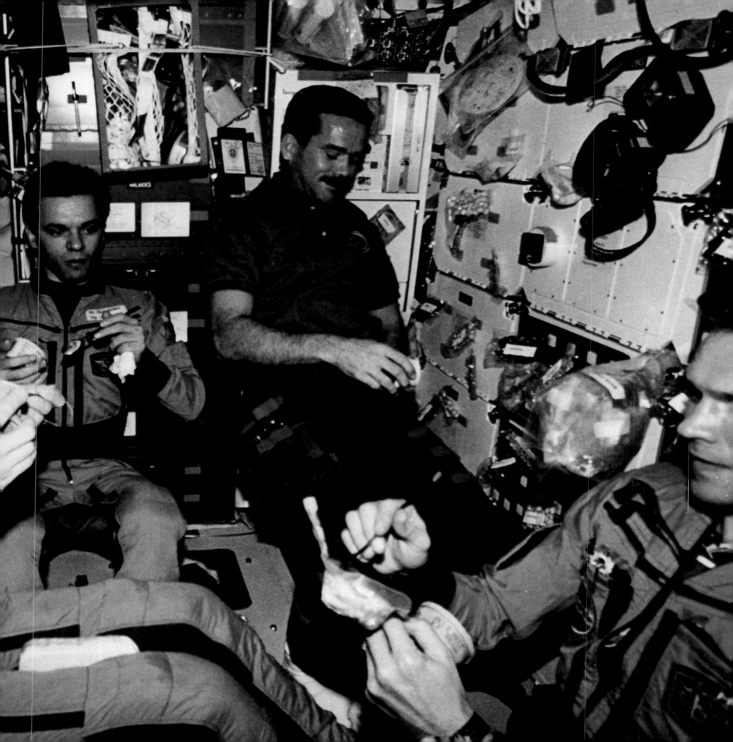

Living in Space

Space stations have a small kitchen and bathroom. Kitchen cabinets hold bags of dried food and juice. Astronauts mix water with the food before they eat. The bathroom has a sink, a toilet, and a shower.

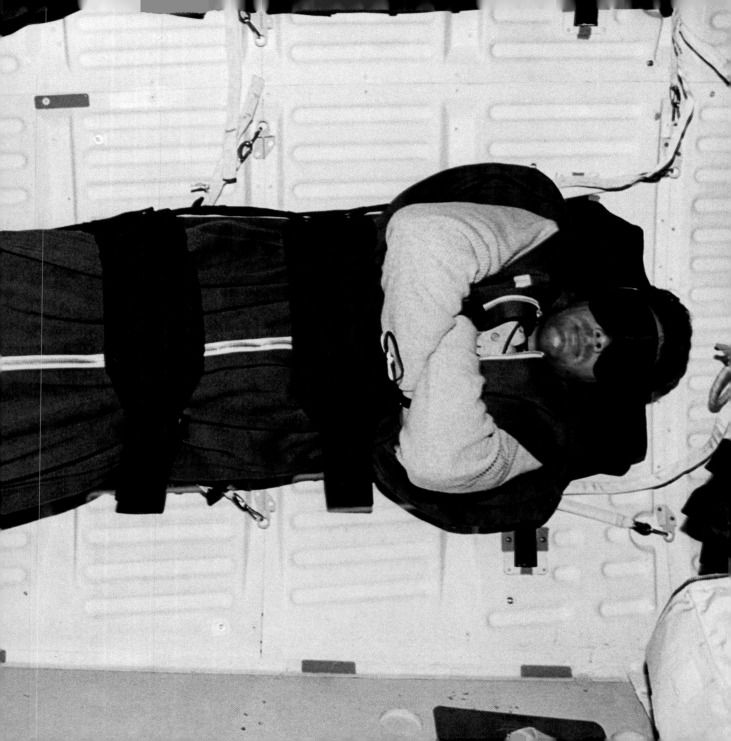

Sleeping in Space

Each astronaut has a small room to sleep in. The astronaut sleeps in a sleeping bag that attaches to a wall. Astronauts do not feel the effects of gravity in space. The sleeping bags keep the astronauts from floating around while they sleep.

gravity
the force that pulls things to Earth; astronauts do not feel the effects of gravity in space stations.

13

Skylab

In 1973, Skylab became the first U.S. space station. Three astronauts could live together inside Skylab for up to three months. Skylab astronauts used a telescope to take pictures of the Sun. Scientists on Earth studied the pictures to learn more about the Sun.

telescope
a tool that makes faraway objects look larger and closer; some space telescopes take pictures.

15

Mir

Russia launched the space station Mir in 1986. Several large sections make up Mir. Cosmonauts can move and reconnect these sections to make the space station different shapes. Different experiments need different laboratory shapes.

cosmonaut
an astronaut from Russia

Nations Working Together

People from many nations are working together to build the International Space Station. Workers build large sections of the station on Earth. Rockets or space shuttles carry these sections into space. Astronauts connect the sections during space walks.

space walk
to work outside a spacecraft while in space; astronauts must wear space suits during space walks.

19

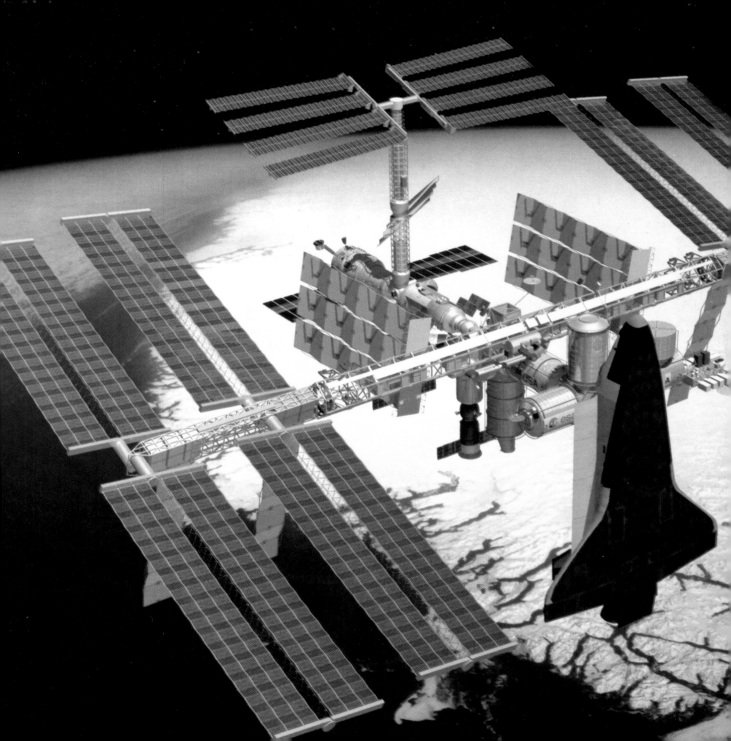